BLOSSOMING 'SHE-EOS' UNLEASHED:

Women Commanding Confidence in the Business World

by

Dr Liz Gilbert

Copyright @ 2024 Dr Liz Gilbert

TABLE OF CONTENTS

A Tribute to Women Who Dare to Dream

This tribute is a recognition and an anthem celebrating the audacity to envision, the resilience to pursue, and the strength to shatter barriers. It is a heartfelt acknowledgment of the women who, in unleashing their inner ambition, become architects of change, pioneers of innovation, and beacons of inspiration.

THE DREAM-WEAVERS

These are the women who, with visionary brilliance, cast their dreams into the cosmos. These are the architects of possibility, the artists sketching futures painted with purpose. Limits do not confine their dreams; they soar beyond the ordinary, sculpting a realm where ambition knows no boundaries.

THE TRAILBLAZERS

We honor the trailblazers who forge paths through uncharted territories. These are the women who, with courage as their compass, navigate the landscapes of challenges and uncertainties. In the symphony of ambition, they are the adventurers, leaving footprints for others to follow. Their journey is a testament to the transformative power of daring to traverse the unknown.

SYMPHONY OF RESILIENCE

It is dedicated to the women who face challenges with an unwavering spirit. These are the orchestrators of tenacity, turning setbacks into stepping stones and setbacks into opportunities for growth. Their resilience is the rhythm that propels the symphony forward, a resounding declaration that women can conquer adversity with unyielding determination.

COLLABORATION CHAMPIONS

The women who understand the strength in unity. Theirs is a narrative of interconnected ambitions, a recognition that success is magnified when shared. This verse lauds the mentors, allies, and collaborators who uplift others, cultivating an ecosystem where every dream is nurtured, and every ambition is amplified.

DIVERSITY DOYENNES

The women who cultivate their ambitions in diverse soils, recognizing the richness that different perspectives bring to the symphony. Their stories are a testament to the beauty of individuality, a celebration of the myriad ways ambition blossoms uniquely in each woman.

LEGACY OF EMPOWERMENT

These are women who carve their stories into the annals of empowerment. Their legacy is not just a professional triumph but a testament to their impact on hearts, minds, and the collective consciousness. This is an ode to the women whose ambition leaves an indelible mark, a legacy that resonates far beyond the present confines.

INTRODUCTION

Hello there!

Welcome to the inspiring Blooming SheEOs Unleashed community! Here, women can confidently explore and conquer the corporate world. Today, more than ever before, women are breaking new ground, pushing boundaries, and taking the helm in entrepreneurship and corporate leadership. We're excited to empower and support you on your journey to success!

During this exciting journey, we will explore the art of networking, the importance of mentorship, and how to maintain a healthy work-life balance.

This book embodies all of the unique characteristics of SheEO, including her power, resilience, and diversity. It is a tribute to the strength that arises when women take control, establish their authority, and inspire others to do the same.

For many SheEOs, this voyage is a chance to explore new horizons, break old habits, and pursue their dreams with unwavering determination.

If you are passionate about promoting diversity and inclusion, have professional experience, or aspire to be an entrepreneur, we welcome you to join us on this exciting journey.

Come with me as we explore the life of SheEO, the ambitious young woman who took charge of her life and positively impacted the thriving success story of the corporate world.

We are delighted to have SheEO on board as a change-maker, trailblazer, and visionary leader in this groundbreaking mission.

"Welcome to the SheEO Unleashed Journey" represents an opportunity to embark on a transformative journey of self-exploration, empowerment, and unwavering commitment to your destiny. It is a portal to a realm where boundless aspiration, steadfast determination, and self-assurance characterize entrepreneurial spirit and corporate leadership.

As this journey proves, all SheEOs possess an inherent talent for decision-making, career-shaping, and self-assurance. The path ahead is an open invitation to survive and flourish, rise to leadership positions, and make a lasting impression on the corporate landscape.

This adventure encourages and celebrates women, guiding them to greater self-assurance and success in a competitive corporate world. Now is the time to embark on an adventure where the possibilities are endless, just like the ambitions of each SheEO.

This manual is more than just a guide; it is an empowerment tool for the SheEO community and a platform for female entrepreneurs to pursue their ambitions. We are all working together to empower ourselves. Members of the Women Entrepreneurs Organization are encouraged to seek their own goals and support and assist other entrepreneurs. Through Unleashed Journey, we can cultivate a culture of empowerment, support, and shared achievement and empower the entire SheEO community.

I sincerely hope that all SheEOs will take this opportunity to cultivate and unleash their boundless ambition so that we can join forces and change the narrative of women in business.

Do you want to unlock the full potential of your ambitions? Then, keep reading because we've got some exciting insights for you on unleashing the power of your inner drive!

CHAPTER 1

Unleashing Her Ambition

Becoming a triumphant SheEO involves personal growth, empowerment, and self-discovery. The key to achieving this starts with reflection, which enables you to pinpoint your objectives and comprehend what propels you toward them.

Take a moment to connect with your aspirations and understand what drives you. This is the first step towards achieving your goals and realizing your dreams. So, let's dive in and explore the roots of your passion!

To conquer your goals, it is essential to fortify your self-assurance and cultivate a growth mindset that perceives obstacles as chances to learn and flourish. We are excited to join you on this empowering expedition towards success!

Just like a garden, a growth mindset requires constant nurturing to bear fruit. With the right mindset, you can turn obstacles into stepping stones and achieve success as a SheEO.

The challenges women entrepreneurs face may seem daunting, but they can overcome them by adopting a growth mindset and using them as opportunities to learn and improve.

To build and maintain ambition, supportive networks are essential. Aspirations do not flourish in a vacuum; they require a collaborative ecosystem to nurture them. A supportive ecosystem, as discussed in the course of this journey, is crucial. A female entrepreneur should surround herself with supportive people who can help her through the challenges of entrepreneurship by serving as a mentor, collaborator, or ally.

In Unleashed Journey, balancing honesty and ambition is never mutually exclusive.

In the face of overwhelming adversity, SheEOs must stay true to their authentic selves while striving for great things. Being genuine helps stay true to one's purpose and positively impacts one's business.

Unleashing the Power of Ambition:

Conquering Impostor Syndrome is a common and significant obstacle that ambitious individuals must overcome. Conquering self-doubt and pursuing their goals requires acknowledging their value and achievements.

Life's journey is a beautiful tapestry, and a powerful thread is waiting to be woven into it—the thread of ambition. It is not just a mere goal but a force that propels you toward a future where your potential knows no bounds. Setting objectives and igniting a fire within yourself will drive you to scale new heights, transcend limits, and create a genuinely extraordinary legacy. I am excited to witness where your ambition will take you and the incredible impact you are destined to make.

Close your eyes for a moment and envision the genesis of your ambition. That spark lights up in the quiet moments of self-reflection and the dreams that dance on the periphery of your consciousness. Ambition is born from the whispers of your aspirations—the yearning for a life that resonates with purpose and fulfillment.

Embracing the Journey:

Ambition is not a fixed goal that you achieve and then stop. It's a continuous journey, an adventure where every step you take contributes to shaping your life story. Embracing challenges, taking risks, and facing uncertainties are all part of this journey. Throughout this odyssey, you will encounter setbacks and failures, temporary obstacles leading to more outstanding successes. Your journey is a testament to your resilience and determination, where each setback serves as a stepping stone to unanticipated triumphs.

A Symphony of Growth:

I'm thrilled to share that your inner ambition is a dynamic and ever-changing river, not a stagnant pool. It's not solely about achieving external goals but constantly evolving and improving oneself. Each life experience and encounter contributes to your personal and professional growth, resulting in a one-of-a-kind melody. I'm excited to see how your journey unfolds, and I'm confident that you'll continue to thrive and achieve great things.

The Power of Self-Belief:

I am excited to share the incredible feeling of unlocking your inner ambition. It's a powerful act that can boost your self-confidence and help you achieve your goals. Shedding doubts and casting aside impostor syndrome can give you the courage to stand tall and embrace your unique talents. Your journey is a testament to the remarkable power within you, reminding you that you are not just a bystander in life's journey but the driving force behind your story. With your unwavering commitment and determination, the possibilities for your future are infinite. Let's embark on this journey together and make your dreams a reality!

Courage to Pursue the Unseen:

Unleashing your inner ambition means having the courage to pursue the unseen and venture into unexplored territories. It's about facing the unknown with a daring spirit and trusting that the canvas for your most extraordinary creations lies within the ambiguity. Your journey is a courageous dance with the unpredictable, a fearless exploration of the vastness within and beyond.

Building Bridges, Not Walls:

Building bridges, not walls, is the art of collaboration. Success is not solitary but communal, and it's about creating connections, fostering relationships, and lifting others as you ascend. Your journey is marked by the bridges you've built, the networks you've nurtured, and the collective strength that propels everyone forward.

Legacy Beyond Numbers:

Ambition is about more than just achieving numerical milestones. It's about crafting a legacy that transcends metrics, impacting hearts, inspiring others, and blazing a trail for those who follow. Your journey is a legacy in the making, a narrative that echoes beyond the confines of conventional success, resonating with the timeless essence of purpose.

In the Realm of Possibility:

Unleashing your inner ambition affirms that the realm of possibility is boundless. It's about stretching the boundaries of your imagination, defying preconceived limitations, and allowing yourself to dream without restraint. Your journey is an exploration of the infinite, a dance with the cosmic possibilities that await those who dare to dream.

Remember that unleashing your inner ambition is not just a destination but a perpetual evolution, a story written with every heartbeat. Your ambition is the guiding star, illuminating the path toward a future where growth knows no bounds, and confidence is an unwavering companion. Embrace the narrative, savor the chapters, and revel in the transformative power of your untamed ambition. This is not just a journey; it's a magnum opus in the making – yours to compose, yours to savor, and yours to shape into an everlasting legacy.

5 APPROACHES TO "OVERCOMING CHALLENGES AND EMBRACING GROWTH"

1. The Growth Mindset Approach:

To make progress and overcome obstacles, it is essential to have a growth mindset. Rather than perceiving failures as barriers, view them as opportunities to learn and grow. Similarly, instead of seeing problems as obstacles, consider them stepping stones towards achieving your goals. Believe that you can continually improve, recover from setbacks, and develop your skills through hard work and focus.

Teach yourself to perceive challenges as opportunities for personal growth and education. Do not regard failures as defeats but as learning experiences that aid your personal and professional development. Foster a commitment to consistently improving yourself. Adopting this mindset empowers you to face challenges head-on and transform them into opportunities for growth.

2. Establishing a Network of Support:

To succeed in business, seeking guidance from those who have been where you're going is essential. You can find mentors or business partners to share their expertise with you. It's also a good idea to connect with other business owners with experience in your field so you can learn from their successes and mistakes.

Networking with successful business people is another excellent way to gain new insights and knowledge. Working with other SheEOs allows you to collaborate and tackle problems more effectively. When you share knowledge and resources, everyone's strengths are magnified, and progress is achieved as a team. Embrace a mentoring and collaborative environment to maximize your potential for success.

3. Build Your Resilience by Hearing Other People's Stories:

Resilience is vital when it comes to overcoming obstacles. One way to gain strength is to hear the experiences of other successful women entrepreneurs or SheEOs. Participation in groups, networks, or events where women openly discuss how they overcame obstacles can be incredibly beneficial. By sharing strategies, coping mechanisms, and practices for building resilience, SheEOs can learn from the experiences of others and cultivate a sense of belonging within their community.

This recognition and honor of resilience helps build unity

and a support system amongst SheEOs during tough

times, reminding each other that they can overcome any

obstacle.

4. Put Your Health First:

Taking care of yourself is crucial for long-term success.

Balancing your career and personal life and ensuring

your goals align with your self-perception is essential.

Prioritize your emotional and physical well-being by

prioritizing self-care and maintaining a good work-life

balance.

When a SheEO has a robust support system, she is better equipped to overcome obstacles and maintain progress over the long term. Maintaining a healthy work-life balance is essential, so give yourself time to care for yourself, spend quality time with loved ones, and do things that bring you joy. Balancing your personal and professional lives is crucial for maintaining resilience and vitality.

Your ability to overcome obstacles is influenced by your mental and physical well-being, so taking care of yourself should be a top priority. By doing so, you can tackle life's challenges with confidence and grace.

5. Continuous Learning and Adaptation:

It is crucial to keep learning in today's ever-changing business world. Adopting a growth mentality and staying updated on developments in your field, new technology, and the constantly evolving dynamics of your market is essential. Keep an open mind, and be willing to modify your plans and strategies when you learn something new or your circumstances change. The ability to adapt quickly to new situations, rebound from setbacks, and drive expansion through well-thought-out decisions are characteristics of a successful SheEO who prioritizes learning.

Embrace the concept of lifelong learning. Stay informed about market trends, technological advancements, and industry developments. To make intelligent decisions, adapt to changing scenarios, and proactively seek growth opportunities, you must prioritize learning. Developing the ability to adjust your plans based on new data and evolving situations is a crucial aspect of agile decision-making. You can remain responsive to the ever-changing business landscape by adopting an elegant decision-making style, enabling you to overcome challenges flexibly.

These strategies provide a strong foundation for a SheEO on the Unleashed Journey to overcome obstacles and embrace change. To succeed and confidently lead in today's dynamic business environment, having a growth mindset, prioritizing mentorship and teamwork, building resilience, taking care of yourself first, and committing to continuous learning are essential.

CHAPTER 2

Leadership Self-Assurance at Its Core

Successful female entrepreneurs possess more than just competence. They have confidence, a game-changer that enables them to confront adversity, inspire those around them, and welcome change with an unwavering resolve. It is important to note that leadership confidence is not the same as arrogance. Instead, it results from self-assurance, the ability to motivate and encourage people around you, and a willingness to take calculated risks.

Being Self-Aware and Reflective:

Embarking on a journey of leadership is an exciting opportunity for self-growth and development. It all starts with self-reflection and acknowledging both your strengths and weaknesses. As a SheEO, it's essential to conduct an honest self-assessment, including your values, goals, and areas for improvement. This insight will enable you to lead authentically, building your leadership confidence.

Authentic leadership is a game-changer in inspiring trust and respect within your team. When you lead authentically, you display honesty, the foundation of trust in any relationship. Your team will be inspired by your genuine approach and follow your lead in being honest and authentic. By embracing your flaws and vulnerabilities, you'll create a positive and welcoming environment where everyone can thrive. So, let's assume this journey with enthusiasm, sincerity, and confidence, knowing that we can positively impact those around us.

The Ability to Recover from Setbacks:

Successful women in executive positions demonstrate incredible self-assurance, a vital quality for achieving greatness. Their confidence in their leadership abilities empowers them to tackle challenges head-on without any hint of fear. They see obstacles as stepping stones to growth and never let them discourage them from their goals. These women possess exceptional analytical and problem-solving skills, which they use to approach complex problems strategically. Their calm demeanor under pressure inspires those around them, building a reputation as influential leaders. It's inspiring to see women with such remarkable qualities leading toward success in the executive world.

Clear and Effective Communication:

Great leaders believe in their vision and inspire their team members to believe it. They are confident in their abilities and communicate their vision clearly and passionately, motivating their team to work towards a common goal. They also understand that outstanding leadership is not one-sided but involves listening to the opinions and feedback of team members. Leaders can foster a welcoming workplace where team members feel valued and empowered by creating a culture of openness and collaboration. When everyone in the team feels heard and understood, they are likelier to work together creatively and collaboratively to achieve the company's objectives. Great leaders know that their vision is only as good as the team that supports it, and they work tirelessly to ensure that each team member feels valued, supported, and empowered to contribute their best work.

Granting Others Agency:

A vital trait of a confident leader is their ability to have unwavering faith in their team members and allow them the freedom to succeed. By doing so, SheEOs impart a sense of appreciation for the unique abilities of each team member and provide them with opportunities to showcase their strengths. This instills a sense of trust among team members, which is crucial in building a strong and self-reliant team.

A self-assured leader always takes advantage of every opportunity to honor and celebrate the achievements of their team members. SheEOs understand the value of recognizing and rewarding effort, which can motivate team members to work more effectively. When people's efforts are acknowledged, it creates a sense of fulfillment, happiness, and motivation in the work environment, which ultimately results in greater productivity.

Continuous Learning and Adaptation:

SheEOs, as female entrepreneurs, are constantly striving to improve their leadership skills and abilities. They recognize that their self-assurance must change as their company environment does. To keep up with the demands of a fast-paced and unpredictable business world, they remain open to new ideas and methods of leadership.

One of the critical ways SheEOs become self-assured leaders is by reflecting on their failures. Instead of seeing failures as setbacks, they view them as opportunities to learn and grow. They reflect on past mistakes and successes to improve their leadership style and continually enhance their skills.

SheEOs possess a unique combination of qualities that contribute to their leadership confidence. These qualities include introspection, perseverance, clear and concise expression of ideas, the ability to inspire others, and a dedication to lifelong education. By committing to and living out these qualities, they can spark revolutionary leadership that changes the face of business forever and embark on the Unleashed Journey.

For visionary leaders like SheEOs, confidence is not just a personality quirk but rather a driving force that propels them forward on their path to empowerment, success, and progress. Their unwavering determination in the face of obstacles bolsters their self-assurance and inspires others to follow their lead.

10 WAYS TO GROW AS A LEADER AND DISPLAY YOUR CAPABILITIES

Female business owners must cultivate and showcase their leadership skills to support their fellow entrepreneurs on the Unleashed Journey. By doing so, they can inspire growth, overcome challenges, and motivate others to achieve their goals. To that end, here are 10 powerful strategies that SheEOs can use to strengthen their leadership abilities and positively impact the entrepreneurial community.

1. Dedicate Resources to Ongoing Education:

In today's fast-paced world, it is imperative to have a continuous learning attitude, especially for leaders. As a leader, you are responsible for guiding your team toward success, and to do that, you must stay updated on the latest trends and best practices in your industry.

One of the best ways to stay current on current trends is to participate in leadership workshops, take classes, and attend relevant events. These opportunities can help you enhance your leadership skills by providing new insights, approaches, and techniques to apply to your work.

Moreover, a dedication to learning demonstrates your adaptability and a quest for information, which are essential traits for effective leadership. It shows that you are open to new ideas and willing to learn from others, which can help you build stronger relationships with your team and foster a culture of continuous improvement.

In addition to attending events and workshops, you can stay current by reading industry publications, following thought leaders on social media, and networking with other professionals in your field. By doing so, you can gain valuable knowledge and insights to help you stay ahead of the curve and make informed decisions.

Being a lifelong student is an essential trait for effective leadership. By fostering a continuous learning attitude and staying up-to-date on current trends, you can enhance your leadership toolbox and demonstrate your adaptability and eagerness to acquire new information.

2. Look for a Mentor and Offer It:

Effective mentorship is a mutually beneficial relationship that can help you grow personally and professionally. As you seek mentors who can guide you and share their experiences, it's important to remember that mentorship is not a one-way street. By also taking on the mentor role, you can develop your leadership abilities and help others flourish.

When searching for a mentor, consider individuals with experience in your field who share your values and goals. A good mentor should be someone you respect and trust, who can provide valuable insights and feedback, and who can help you navigate challenges and opportunities.

It's also important to be open to mentoring others, regardless of their field of work or level of experience. Mentoring others can help you refine your skills and knowledge and be a rewarding way to give back to your community.

When mentoring others, focus on building a relationship based on trust and mutual respect. Listen actively to their concerns and goals and provide constructive feedback and guidance. Please encourage them to take risks, learn from their mistakes, and celebrate their accomplishments.

Two-way mentoring is a valuable tool for personal and professional growth. By finding mentors who can guide you and becoming a mentor to others, you can develop your leadership abilities, build valuable relationships, and contribute to the success of your community.

3. Display Resilience in the Face of Adversity:
Leaders who prioritize empathy can establish strong bonds with their team members and create a culture of collaboration, trust, and respect. By demonstrating an

understanding of their team's emotions, needs, and aspirations, leaders can build a safe and inclusive workplace where everyone feels valued and supported. They can also leverage empathy to enhance their decision-making ability, build consensus, and resolve conflicts effectively. A leader who leads with empathy can inspire their team to achieve greater heights and drive outstanding results.

4. Improve Your Communication Skills:
Effective communication is the foundation of a successful team. It is the key to inspiring and motivating your team to be their best. By being transparent, engaging, and attentive in your communication, you can foster an environment of trust, respect, and collaboration. When everyone on your team feels heard and valued,

they are more likely to contribute their ideas, share their concerns, and work together towards achieving their goals.

It is essential to articulate your ideas clearly to enhance your communication skills. This means being concise, yet thorough, in your messaging. It also means using engaging stories and examples to help your team connect with your message. By sharing relatable experiences, you can help your team better understand your perspective and how it relates to their work.

Additionally, it is important to listen attentively to your team's feedback. By actively seeking and considering their input, you can create a culture of open communication and trust. When your team feels heard and appreciated, they are more likely to be motivated and engaged.

So why wait? Start building communication skills today and unleash your team's potential. With effective communication, you can create a more informed, united, and prosperous team!

5. Show the Way:

As a leader, you must show confidence in your decisions and actions. It would be best if you led your team by example, demonstrating the values of honesty and responsibility in all you do. By owning your decisions and actions, you affirm that you are reliable, dependable, and trustworthy.

Fostering a culture of honesty and responsibility within your team is essential. If your team members see that you are committed to these values, they are more likely to follow suit. Creating a culture of openness and accountability can improve communication, increase trust, and ultimately drive better results.

In today's business world, ethical conduct and professionalism are more important than ever. By leading with honesty and responsibility, you can set yourself apart as a leader committed to doing what is right, even when difficult. So, take the initiative and lead confidently, knowing that your team and the business world will respect and admire you for it.

6. Promote Teamwork and Broad Participation:

In a team, inclusive leadership plays a critical role in promoting teamwork and welcoming all members regardless of their background. It entails embracing different perspectives and ideas and creating an atmosphere where every individual's opinion is valued and respected. This approach fosters a culture of open communication, trust, and mutual respect, which improves team dynamics and allows everyone to contribute their unique talents and capabilities to achieve shared goals.

By being inclusive, leaders demonstrate their commitment to diversity and inclusion, crucial values in today's diverse and interconnected world. They recognize and appreciate each team member's differences and harness these differences to create a more innovative and effective team. Inclusivity also promotes a sense of belonging, which increases engagement and motivation, leading to higher productivity and job satisfaction.

Overall, inclusive leadership is a powerful tool for creating a positive and collaborative work environment that brings out the best in everyone, promotes teamwork, and drives success.

7. Work on your ability to make decisions:

To make effective strategic decisions, gathering as much information as possible is essential. This includes analyzing data, assessing risks, considering potential obstacles, and weighing the potential benefits of different options. Additionally, it's crucial to remain focused on the organization's larger goals rather than getting bogged down in details or short-term considerations. By maintaining a big-picture perspective, you'll be better equipped to make decisions that align with the organization's overall strategy and drive progress toward long-term success.

Remember, effective decision-making is a crucial component of effective leadership - and the ability to think strategically is a valuable asset in any professional setting.

8. Recognize and Respond to New Developments:

Effective leadership involves the incredible power of clear communication and the ability to motivate others to take action. Setting well-defined goals and expectations and providing constructive feedback can inspire your team members to achieve great things. Fostering an open and honest environment that values diverse perspectives and encourages collaboration is essential. Leading by example and recognizing the contributions of your team members builds trust and creates a positive work culture. Always remember that leadership is not about controlling people but supporting and nurturing them to reach their full potential. With your guidance, your team can achieve incredible success.

9. Efficiently Assign Tasks:

To delegate tasks effectively, it's important first to assess the strengths and weaknesses of your team members. Once you clearly understand their abilities, you can assign tasks they are best suited for. This ensures that the job is done well and helps build their confidence and sense of ownership.

It's also essential to communicate your expectations for each task. Provide clear instructions, deadlines, and necessary resources to ensure that your team members have everything they need to complete the job. This will help avoid confusion and ensure everyone is working towards the same goal.

Delegation can be a powerful tool for leaders, allowing them to focus on their areas of expertise while also developing the skills and talents of their team members. Empowering your team through delegation creates a more collaborative and productive work environment that benefits everyone involved.

10. Recognize Achievements and 'Festivize' Them:

In the journey towards becoming successful SheEOs, it's important to remember that demonstrating leadership skills is not just about delegating tasks and making decisions. It's also about creating a positive work environment where employees feel appreciated and motivated to achieve their best.

One way to achieve this is by acknowledging and celebrating your team's successes. You can do this in various ways, such as through verbal praise, written recognition, or even small rewards. By celebrating successes, you create a culture of positivity, which in turn encourages your team to work harder and achieve more.

Another critical tactic for SheEOs is to develop emotional intelligence. Emotional intelligence is the ability to understand and manage one's own emotions, as well as the feelings of others. By developing emotional intelligence, SheEOs can create a more empathetic and compassionate workplace, which leads to more effective communication and collaboration.

In conclusion, becoming a successful SheEO requires adopting specific tactics beyond making decisions and delegating tasks. It involves creating a positive work environment, developing emotional intelligence, and celebrating successes. By adopting these tactics, SheEOs can build a strong team, foster a culture of positivity, and achieve their full potential as leaders.

CHAPTER 3

Developing the Capacity of Women in Executive Roles

Successful leadership involves the ability to make bold decisions and the skills to navigate uncertainty and take calculated risks. The Unleashed Journey of Female Entrepreneurs emphasizes the importance of decision-making skills for women entrepreneurs in today's fast-paced business world. To succeed as a leader, refining your decision-making skills and developing the confidence to take calculated risks is crucial.

One key aspect of making fearless decisions is embracing the unknown. SheEOs recognize that every choice involves some degree of uncertainty and that uncertainty can be an opportunity rather than a roadblock. By viewing uncertainty as a chance for improvement, leaders can inspire their teams and create a culture of innovation and adaptability.

In addition to embracing uncertainty, leaders must also be able to make quick decisions. SheEOs demonstrate their leadership abilities by evaluating challenges, gathering relevant data, and making swift judgments. Decisiveness is a leadership quality that sets the standard for a creative and adaptable work environment. When a leader is decisive, the team trusts their abilities and feels confident in their direction.

But making bold decisions and taking calculated risks requires more than just confidence and quick thinking. It also requires a willingness to learn from failure and adapt to changing circumstances. SheEOs who recognize and learn from their mistakes are better equipped to make bold decisions and take their organizations to new heights.

Successful leadership requires a combination of bold decision-making, calculated risk-taking, and adaptability in the face of uncertainty. By honing your decision-making skills, embracing the unknown, and learning from your mistakes, you can become a more effective leader and drive your organization toward success.

Effective leadership requires making fearless decisions that align with the organization's goals and objectives. SheEOs are responsible for making critical decisions based on a strategic vision aligning with the company's objectives. They must lead by example and make decisions consistent with their strategic vision to inspire their team members to work together to achieve the organization's vision.

To achieve fearless decision-making, SheEOs must adopt a data-driven strategy involving calculated risks. They collect and analyze data to comprehensively understand the business environment, including market trends and customer behavior. This information helps them identify opportunities and make informed decisions that align with the company's objectives.

SheEOs proactively identify potential risks and develop contingency plans to mitigate the risks. They take calculated risks that align with their strategic vision and goals and are not afraid to pivot their strategy if necessary. They effectively balance the need for risk-taking with stability and consistency to create a cohesive and successful organization.

SheEOs make fearless decisions by adopting a data-driven strategy that includes taking calculated risks. They analyze data to gain insights into the business environment and identify opportunities. They balance the need for risk-taking with stability and consistency to achieve their strategic vision and organizational objectives.

Successful entrepreneurship requires a willingness to learn from failures and make fearless decisions. Female entrepreneurs know that failures are inevitable but don't shy away from them. Instead, they embrace failures as opportunities to gain insights and learn from mistakes. They use setbacks to reflect on what went wrong and adjust to grow as leaders. Female entrepreneurs take calculated risks based on their experience and knowledge and don't hesitate to take responsibility when things don't work out.

Transparency is a crucial aspect of fearless decision-making for female entrepreneurs. They understand the importance of being transparent with their team members. They provide background information and reasoning behind their decisions, creating trust and connection between team members and corporate goals. They believe that transparency leads to better communication and opens the door for constructive feedback from team members.

Regardless of the outcome, taking ownership of decisions is a crucial component of fearless decision-making. Female entrepreneurs know that taking responsibility for their actions builds integrity and trust among their team members. They don't shy away from accountability and instead set an example for their team members. Demonstrating accountability fosters a culture of responsibility and support in the workplace.

Female entrepreneurs take a proactive approach to failures, embrace transparency in their decision-making process, and take ownership of their decisions to create a constructive and supportive work environment.

Making fearless decisions is vital for any leader, particularly for SheEOs who guide their organizations toward success. To make such decisions, a SheEO must balance relying on their intuition and conducting a thorough analysis. Their instinct, honed after years of practice, acts as their compass, providing a human touch that adds a distinct viewpoint to their decision-making process. While data and analysis are helpful, a leader's intuition plays a crucial role in shaping their decision-making skills.

To promote a culture of innovation, a SheEO must encourage their team to take measured risks and give them a voice in finding solutions. By working together, they can foster confidence in taking risks, leading to more innovative solutions. Encouraging risk-taking also means embracing the possibility of failure, which can be a valuable learning experience for everyone involved.

Moreover, courageous decision-making is a hallmark of effective leadership, and SheEOs are no exception. By making bold choices, they can steer their organizations toward success, even amid uncertainty and obstacles. SheEOs foster an environment that rewards measured risks and encourages proactive thinking, praising, and learning from examples of bravery.

In the Unleashed Journey, courageous decision-making is a game-changing tactic for SheEOs to hone and display their leadership abilities. It requires a mindset willing to push the organization toward success while navigating uncertainties. SheEOs' leadership legacy is characterized by bold decision-making, which they demonstrate through their strategic vision, open communication, accountability, and dedication to learning.

ENHANCING SELF-ASSURANCE IN DECISION-MAKING: INVESTIGATIVE APPROACHES FOR WOMEN IN EXECUTIVE POSITIONS

Embarking on the journey of entrepreneurship can be both challenging and rewarding. As SheEOs, it's essential to have confidence in our decision-making abilities. A great leader can make well-informed judgments without hesitation. That's why I've developed 5 exploratory strategies to help SheEOs cultivate and showcase their self-assurance in decision-making. We can approach our entrepreneurial ventures with enthusiasm, optimism, and positivity with these tools.

1. Comprehensive Educational Encounters:

As a SheEO, it is essential to continuously improve your decision-making skills to ensure that your business stays competitive and relevant in today's fast-paced market. One way to do this is by participating in executive education programs that provide hands-on, experiential learning opportunities. These programs offer a variety of resources, including interactive seminars, simulated scenarios, and real-world case studies that can help you practice and hone your strategic decision-making skills in a safe setting.

In addition to these programs, gaining expertise in your field is essential. You can learn about your industry, including its trends, challenges, and opportunities. One way to gain knowledge is by participating in industry forums, attending conferences, and talking to influential people in your field. By delving into the complexities of your industry, you may boost your decision-making confidence and make well-informed choices based on a solid grasp of the business landscape.

Moreover, staying up-to-date with your industry's latest technologies and innovations is essential. This can help you make informed decisions regarding using new tools and strategies in your business. You can also network with other experts and thought leaders in your field to gain insights into emerging trends and best practices.

By participating in executive education programs, gaining expertise in your field, and staying up-to-date with the latest technologies and innovations, you can improve your decision-making skills as a SheEO and stay ahead of the competition in today's rapidly evolving business landscape.

2. The Role of Peer Networks and Mentors:

It's always a good idea to seek advice from successful leaders with a wealth of experience and a track record of making sound decisions. By learning from their experiences and seeking guidance, you can gain valuable insights to help you feel more confident about your abilities.

One great way to connect with other female entrepreneurs and leaders is by joining a peer network or mastermind group. These groups offer a supportive environment where members can discuss challenges, share ideas, and give and receive feedback. By working together in this way, you can build your skills and confidence and gain the tools you need to tackle challenging problems. Whether you're just starting or an experienced entrepreneur, joining a peer network or mastermind group can be a valuable investment in your professional development.

3. Exercises in Simulated Decision-Making:

Participating in decision-making simulations that reflect your company's real-world situations is essential. By gaining hands-on experience, SheEOs can enhance their decision-making abilities in a controlled environment, allowing them to tackle actual problems better.

You should attend interactive workshops focusing on developing your sound decision-making ability. These workshops can include group projects, case studies, and guided conversations. Participating in these activities provides a lively setting to test different decision-making methods and gain confidence through practical experience.

4. Feedback Mechanisms with Multiple Facets:

Consider implementing a system of 360-degree feedback in your company. Seek input from everyone, not just your bosses and colleagues. This comprehensive feedback process provides diverse perspectives on your decision-making abilities, which can help you improve and gain confidence.

Additionally, consider conducting post-decision reviews for significant choices. Reflect on the outcomes, seek opinions from your team members, and evaluate how you arrived at your decisions. By comprehending the impact of your choices and learning from your experiences, you can enhance your confidence in future decision-making situations.

5. Ways to Foster Your Growth and Mindfulness:

Are you feeling overwhelmed and looking for an opportunity to escape it all? Then why not consider attending a leadership retreat that emphasizes self-improvement and mindfulness? These retreats provide a unique chance for SheEOs to step back from their busy lives, reflect on their leadership style, establish their principles, and practice mindfulness.

At these retreats, participants engage in various activities designed to help them better understand themselves and their leadership style. Through workshops, group discussions, and one-on-one mentoring, you learn to identify your strengths and weaknesses, set achievable goals, and develop effective strategies to reach them.

They also receive guidance on cultivating a more mindful approach to decision-making, which can help them stay focused and make better choices under pressure.

One of the critical elements of these retreats is the emphasis on mindfulness practices. Participants are encouraged to dedicate each day to meditation and other mindfulness exercises, which can help them improve their concentration, reduce stress, and stay calm and composed in difficult situations.

By participating in these retreats, successful women in executive roles can consciously develop and exhibit self-assurance in their decision-making abilities. Through simulated exercises, mentorship, diverse learning experiences, feedback mechanisms, and personal development practices, participants learn to gain the trust of their teams and organizations. This approach can help them become more effective leaders, build stronger relationships, and achieve tremendous success in their professional and personal lives.

CHAPTER 4

Networking Like a Pro

Networking has become crucial to making informed decisions in today's rapidly changing entrepreneurial world. Also, it involves more than just building relationships - it is a complex process that fosters teamwork, encourages diverse perspectives, and provides valuable information to boost the confidence of SheEOs while making decisions.

This is where expanding perspectives come in. By networking, you can interact with individuals from various backgrounds, professions, and industries. To broaden their horizons, challenge their assumptions, and gain new ideas, SheEOs should connect with experts outside their expertise. Hearing multiple perspectives is beneficial when making decisions, allowing for a more well-rounded and informed choice.

Networking is a two-way street that allows for the exchange of information and insights. As a community, SheEOs can learn from each other's experiences, opinions, and strategies for decision-making. Networking results in solid decision-making skills, making it an excellent source of continuous learning through knowledge sharing.

You can form collaborations, partnerships, and alliances through networking. This establishes a foundation for

SheEOs to connect with experts whose knowledge and experience can complement their own. By doing so, they can pave the way for group decision-making, improving the quality and efficiency of their decisions.

Networking also helps SheEOs to find mentors who can provide guidance when faced with difficult decisions. Building relationships with mentors can give them valuable insights and equip them to handle complex situations confidently.

SheEOs can stay up-to-date with the latest trends, market data, and emerging technologies within their industry circle through networking. Constant access to data allows them to plan for the future of their industries in a way that takes advantage of both present and future trends.

Making well-informed decisions is a significant benefit of maintaining contact.

The entrepreneurial journey can be challenging, but networking provides an inherent support system. SheEOs can build emotional resilience and support by sharing their experiences with their network. Receiving support and guidance during difficult times can help them develop a mindset that can confidently make decisions when faced with pressure.

Networking events offer SheEOs opportunities to showcase their knowledge and skills and gain self-assurance by speaking publicly and taking the lead. Such events help SheEOs to establish connections, secure funds, and reach potential investors. By networking with individuals with similar interests, SheEOs can increase their financial leverage, which is essential for driving growth and making strategic decisions.

Active networking also enables SheEOs to create a solid personal brand, gain recognition in their sector, and shape positive perceptions and industry narratives. It equips them with the flexibility to deal with the unknowns in a business world that is constantly evolving. Networking provides them with the insights necessary to identify early warning signs of changes in their industry and put their businesses in the best possible position for success.

Networking is a multi-dimensional talent that can help SheEOs make better decisions. It involves connecting with others, sharing knowledge, working together, being mentored, gaining insight into the industry, receiving emotional support, building confidence, securing funding, enhancing brand visibility, and adaptability. As their networks expand, SheEOs build a strong foundation of support, expertise, and self-assurance that helps them navigate the ever-changing world of entrepreneurship.

BUILDING AN EFFECTIVE PROFESSIONAL NETWORK: AN ALL-INCLUSIVE RESOURCE FOR WOMEN IN EXECUTIVE POSITIONS

Building a robust professional network is crucial for SheEOs to succeed in the constantly changing world of entrepreneurship. Cultivating and maintaining an extensive network provides various benefits, including accessing a vast pool of support, ideas, and knowledge. If you are a SheEO and wish to build and leverage your professional network to your advantage, follow this road map:

Define Your Networking Objectives:

Before engaging in any networking activities, make sure your objectives are clear. Having a specific goal in mind can help you make more meaningful connections and achieve your networking goals, whether finding a mentor, learning more about your business, or looking for ways to collaborate.

Develop a Genuine Personal Brand:

Be genuine and consistent in building your brand to reflect your values and professional persona. A strong brand is produced by constant offline and online activity. A clearly defined personal brand helps attract like-minded individuals and build credibility within your network.

Attend Trade Shows and Conventions:

Attend industry-specific events such as conferences and seminars to network extensively. These events provide an excellent opportunity to meet influential people in your field and establish connections that could lead to future collaborations. Participate in conversations, attend seminars, and maximize opportunities to share knowledge.

Utilize Online Resources:

Create a robust online presence using channels like LinkedIn, Twitter, and industry forums. Create an impressive web profile that showcases your skills, goals, and achievements. Expand your digital reach by actively participating in relevant discussions, sharing valuable content, and connecting with professionals.

Find a Mentor and Offer Mentorship:

Encourage mentorship between seasoned professionals and those just starting their careers. A mentorship program that works both ways can help you build more robust professional and personal networks while expanding your horizons intellectually.

Expand Your Network Across Industries:

Build a diverse network that goes beyond your current field. Engage in conversations with experts from other fields to expand your horizons and challenge your thinking. Having a varied network makes your company more resilient and provides more perspectives on the strategies and problems you face.

Attend social gatherings and networking events:

Participating in casual meetups, social gatherings, and networking mixers is a great way to connect with people in a relaxed environment. Strike conversations with professionals from various fields, share your experiences and get to know them better.

Join professional groups:

Joining groups that focus on your industry or becoming a professional association member can provide you with access to exclusive events, forums, and networking opportunities. This is an excellent way to meet people with similar interests and professional backgrounds.

Cultivate relationships:

After making initial contacts, it's essential to maintain communication. Share relevant materials, express gratitude, and suggest ideas for collaboration. Consistent follow-up is vital to building lasting partnerships.

Participate in group efforts:

Collaborate with others in your community by exchanging ideas, assets, and opportunities. Be recognized for making a positive impact and working together with others. Giving back to your network improves your professional standing and the quality of your professional community.

Attend workshops to improve your skills:

Participating in industry-specific skill-building courses and workshops is an effective way to hone your professional abilities while meeting like-minded people.

Consider advisory positions:

Being part of advisory boards or committees relevant to your area of expertise can establish you as an industry leader and provide valuable networking opportunities. Advisory responsibilities can open doors to collaboration and networking opportunities.

Keep an open mind and be flexible:

In the corporate world, networking tactics must be flexible since things constantly change. Therefore, embracing change, being open to new things, and staying relaxed is essential. To keep your network responsive to changes in the industry, you must be willing to adapt.

Go to Regional Business Gatherings:

Participating in chamber of commerce activities and local business forums is an excellent way to engage with the community and network with entrepreneurs, company executives, and community influencers.

Capitalize on Your Alumni Network:

Reach out to the alum networks of the schools or programs you attended. Numerous alumni networks exist worldwide, serving as excellent resources for making contacts, finding mentors, and working together.

Establish an Alliance of Advocates:

Find people in your network who can advocate and champion your cause. The backing of these champions can enhance your exposure, credibility, and access to influential people. Establishing a network of advocates may increase your impact in the business world.

Volunteer Your Time:

Participate in charitable endeavors and volunteer work for the betterment of your community. Giving back has a multiplicative effect: it improves society and connects you with others who share your values of social responsibility.

Evaluate and Enhance Your Computer Network:

Assess the effectiveness of your network regularly. Identify the relationships that have led to successful partnerships and the ones that need work. Periodically assess your career objectives and adjust your network to stay on track.

Networking Properly Is Crucial:

Maintain proper networking etiquette by being respectful, polite, and aware of professional standards. Maintain professionalism in all online or offline contacts and respond promptly to messages.

Keep a Positive Image Online:

Consistently maintain a professional image in your online presence to create a positive brand. Post uplifting content regularly, engage in conversations and update your profiles. Presenting yourself positively online reflects in your professional network.

Building a robust professional network is an ongoing process that demands constant attention to detail, collaboration, and learning. A comprehensive and well-planned network is a potent tool for female entrepreneurs, empowering them to face challenges confidently, make astute decisions, and achieve lasting success in the ever-evolving business world. These all-inclusive strategies will assist women entrepreneurs in establishing and maintaining a valuable network as they progress in their careers and assume leadership roles in their respective fields.

OVERCOMING OBSTACLES: PAVING THE WAY WITH INFLUENTIAL PROFESSIONAL NETWORKS

The term "glass ceiling" describes the invisible barriers women face in the workplace, particularly in the realm of female entrepreneurship. These barriers can create obstacles for women looking to climb the corporate ladder or advance in their careers. Women entrepreneurs face unique challenges, including limited access to funding, lack of mentorship opportunities, and societal biases against their leadership abilities.

To overcome these barriers, female entrepreneurs can adopt several strategies. One of the most effective approaches is to build a solid professional network. Networking can help women entrepreneurs access valuable resources, including mentorship, funding, and business opportunities. It can also provide them with a supportive community of like-minded professionals who can offer guidance, advice, and encouragement.

By building a solid network, women entrepreneurs can overcome the glass ceiling and shatter it. They can gain the confidence and resources they need to reach new heights in their careers and significantly impact their industries.

Glass ceilings are invisible impediments that hinder women's advancement in leadership positions. To overcome these obstacles, SheEOs can cultivate a solid professional network to introduce them to resources, opportunities, and influential persons who can encourage and inspire them.

Strategic Networking for Professional

SheEOs can strategically utilize their contacts for professional growth by actively networking. Networking with influential people in their fields and seeking mentors who can help them succeed can help them overcome the obstacles often associated with the glass ceiling.

A diversified professional network helps break down prejudices and exposes people to new ideas. By reaching out to people from all walks of life, SheEOs hope to break down stereotypes and promote inclusive leadership, ultimately leading to a workplace that values and embraces diversity.

Mentorship as a Means to Progress:

Mentoring can lead to significant career advancement when part of an influential professional network. The advice, stories, and insights seasoned mentors offer can be invaluable in shattering the glass ceiling. Having a mentor can provide SheEOs with the support, guidance, and self-assurance they need to tackle systemic issues. Achieving Systemic Change through Collective Empowerment:

A solid professional network is more than just for personal achievement; it can be used as a platform for group empowerment and structural transformation. The collective impact of a network of SheEOs can change attitudes and practices within the sector, combat prejudice, and break down the glass ceiling that prevents more women from achieving leadership positions.

Strong networks provide entrepreneurial women with access to strategic partnerships and opportunities to expand their businesses. By collaborating with influential industry members, women-led firms can increase the influence of their endeavors and overcome traditional growth obstacles.

The information gap creates a fertile ground for the glass ceiling, which can be overcome by knowledge networks that facilitate informed decision-making. The best way for SheEOs to stay up-to-date with industry news, trends, and best practices is to join a solid professional network that promotes information sharing. Knowledge networks enable informed decision-making, which drives success by removing obstacles.

As I reflect on the growing trend of women taking up leadership positions and spearheading mentorship programs, I am filled with awe and admiration. The idea of women helping other women by sharing their knowledge, skills, and experiences is nothing short of fantastic. It is not only a powerful way to address gender inequality and level the playing field in the corporate world but also a way to create a ripple effect of change that will benefit future generations.

Such mentorship programs are crucial in building a more inclusive and diverse workplace where women can feel valued, supported, and empowered to achieve their goals. These programs provide a safe space for SheEOs to share their experiences, receive guidance and support, and gain access to valuable networking opportunities that can help them advance in their careers.

I am confident these programs will foster a bright and inclusive future for all aspiring leaders, regardless of gender. By working together and supporting each other, we can create a world where women in leadership positions are the norm, not the exception. So, let's roll up our sleeves and make it happen!

The inspiring SheEOs are harnessing the power of their networks to ignite change and promote gender equality. With enthusiasm and confidence, they are fully engaged in meaningful discussions, projects, and policies to level the playing field and shatter the glass ceiling. Their cheerful and friendly approach is sure to make a lasting impact.

Women in executive positions understand the significance of fostering a robust professional network.

This pursuit is not just limited to advancing their career but can also bring life-changing opportunities by breaking down barriers. As SheEO, these women achieve personal success and positively impact the world by actively networking, seeking mentorship, forming alliances, advocating for gender equality, and promoting collective empowerment. Breaking through the glass ceiling signifies the strength, impact, and determination of women in leadership positions who fearlessly pave new paths with the support of their professional networks. It is truly inspiring to see women empowering one another and achieving great things together.

CHAPTER 5

Challenging Gender Stereotypes

A critical step in achieving gender parity and breaking glass ceilings is combating and eliminating gender stereotypes in the corporate sphere. As pioneers in entrepreneurship, SheEOs are crucial in dispelling these prejudices, changing people's views, and creating a culture where competence, experience, and leadership abilities take precedence over rigid gender roles.

Gender stereotypes are long-held cultural views about the proper responsibilities and personal qualities of men and women. These gender stereotypes show up as assumptions about how people should be led, how good they are at making decisions, and whether or not they are suited for specific jobs in the corporate sector.

Through SheEOs become influential change agents through female leadership roles, leading by example. In addition to being a personal victory, their capacity to combat and dismantle gender stereotypes has a revolutionary impact on the corporate world. The efforts of SheEOs lead to a more welcoming and equal workplace for all employees.

By prioritizing competence, abilities, and experience over conventional gender standards, SheEOs work to dismantle gender preconceptions. Redefining the traits associated with successful leaders, SheEOs break away

from confining stereotypes by demonstrating their

effectiveness in decision-making, strategic planning, and

visionary leadership.

One way that SheEOs help break down preconceptions is

by promoting various leadership styles inside their

organizations. Recognizing that gender is not a limiting

factor in good leadership, they advocate for a diverse

leadership team to help create an inclusive space where

people of all genders can shine.

Encouraging inclusive workplace cultures is critical for

SheEOs to promote equality at every level. Gender is not

a barrier to success because they are staunch advocates

for diversity and equality throughout the company. A

culture of equal opportunity and eliminating prejudice are

two outcomes of inclusive policies that seep into an organization's fabric.

Women in executive positions combat gender stereotypes by empowering women to dream big, participating in mentoring programs, and functioning as examples for ambitious professionals. Dismantling gender preconceptions that claim certain leadership roles are reserved for specific genders is done by promoting the achievements of SheEOs, sharing their experiences, and offering advice. Gender biases can be removed through mentorship.

Inspiring a new generation of female executives to chase ambitious goals regardless of societal expectations, SheEOs share their tales of conquering obstacles, shattering barriers, and achieving the peak of their professions.

By aggressively addressing unconscious workplace biases, SheEOs educate and sensitize their colleagues. They aim to reduce bias in employee performance reviews by raising awareness about stereotypes' role in the decision-making process and providing resources to help people overcome their prejudices.

By developing collaborative networks, SheEOs utilize their established professional networks to empower other women. Through networking, people can work together, receive encouragement, and strengthen their communities, thereby disproving gender preconceptions by fostering communities where women can share experiences, gain knowledge, and advance professionally.

SheEOs advocate for systemic change and actively shape policies and practices. One way to do this is by affecting norms and policies that reinforce harmful gender stereotypes. Contributing to a corporate landscape where individuals are judged based on their abilities and accomplishments, regardless of gender, SheEOs participate in industry-wide initiatives and use their positions to push change.

To achieve gender parity and smash glass ceilings, it is crucial to dismantle gender preconceptions in the corporate sphere. SheEOs spearhead this change because of their dedication, tenacity, and leadership abilities. Women in executive positions fight gender stereotypes in their respective fields and beyond by mentoring, activism, and taking action. They are part of a more significant movement that hopes for a workplace free of gender bias where women and men are valued for their strengths. By doing so, SheEOs create space for a more inclusive and equitable future while redefining leadership.

THE SHEEO: A LIGHT TO EMPOWER OTHERS AND BREAK DOWN GENDER BARRIERS

For SheEOs fighting to eliminate gender bias and promote diversity and inclusion in the workplace, the power to empower others is a fundamental value. This dedication goes beyond just achieving one's own goals; it serves as a compass for SheEOs to mentor and inspire those around them, setting in motion a chain reaction that breaks down barriers of gender and initiates a sea change in the business world.

Leadership as a Driver of Trans-formative Change:

SheEOs set the tone for empowerment inside their organizations due to their leadership roles. By employing inclusive leadership approaches, they foster an atmosphere where people of all genders feel safe enough to share their expertise and ideas.

Using Mentorship to Bring About Change:

Mentorship can change lives, and SheEOs understand this. They help shape the leaders of tomorrow by sharing their experiences, wisdom, and experiences in mentoring programs and paving the way for their success. When it comes to combating gender stereotypes and encouraging career advancement, this mentoring philosophy becomes an indispensable tool.

Collaborative Empowerment:

SheEOs promote an environment where people support and encourage one another. They build a community where everyone feels appreciated by encouraging cooperation and mutual assistance. This cooperative attitude stands in opposition to preconceptions that prioritize individualism over teamwork.

Offering Fair Chances:

Ensuring everyone has an equal chance to succeed is integral to practicing meritocracy. Instead of basing promotions and pay raises on a person's gender, SheEOs advocate for a meritocratic system that rewards people for their performance. A dedication to equity like this fights against prejudices that prevent certain people from reaching their full potential.

Diversity in Leadership Styles:

SheEOs wholeheartedly embrace and support a variety of leadership approaches. In doing so, they help dismantle gender stereotypes about how leaders should act by highlighting and appreciating the distinct contributions of all team members. The end product is a leadership landscape that is both more diverse and more vibrant.

Funding Career Advancement:

The act of investing in the professional growth of others is empowering them, which in turn enhances their skills. SheEOs promote and facilitate learning opportunities, education, and skill development. This dedication can help others and disprove gender stereotypes by demonstrating that learning new things is essential for people of both genders.

Building Exposure Platforms:

SheEOs aims to make sure that all opinions are heard by actively building platforms that do just that. They ensure that no one is undervalued or ignored because of their gender by giving everyone chances to show off their skills, ideas, and accomplishments. When people can be seen, it helps them break down barriers and misconceptions.

Cry for a Better Work-Life Balance:

SheEOs understand the significance of a healthy work-life balance for promoting well-being. They combat preconceptions that could restrict some people due to social expectations by fighting for legislation that encourages flexible work arrangements and puts health first. This dedication helps create an environment where all employees can succeed.

Building Relationships for Growth:

Leveraging their networks to empower others, SheEOs expand their horizons. They help people in their professional circles succeed by introducing them to valuable contacts, opportunities, and resources. Networking is a powerful tool that connects people, empowers them, tears down boundaries, and combats prejudices.

Advocates for Corporate Social Responsibility:

Outside of the Boardroom: Assisting others goes beyond only the professional sphere; it's a dedication to doing good in the world. Beyond gender stereotypes and reflecting a more significant commitment to empowerment, SheEOs advocate activities that contribute to the well-being of communities. Their good influence goes beyond words and impact.

Finally, beyond individual achievement, the impact of SheEOs' dedication to uplifting others is profound. Contributing to a cultural transformation in the business sector, SheEOs aggressively challenge gender stereotypes, develop mentorship, promote collaboration, and champion equitable opportunity. By working together to empower others, we can break down barriers and leave a legacy of inclusive leadership, resilience, and prosperity for future generations.

CHAPTER 6

Mentorship and the Next Generation's Empowerment

Mentorship and enabling the next generation form a symbiotic relationship crucial for sustainable growth in the dynamic corporate world. Mentorship is essential to the progress of organizations and societies, not only the development of individuals inside them. Because of their pioneering spirit, SheEOs understand the critical importance of mentoring new leaders and work tirelessly to facilitate this relationship.

Acquiring New Knowledge and Enhancing Existing Abilities:

Mentorship facilitates the transmission of information and skills from experienced professionals, like SheEOs, to the next generation, thus passing along wisdom. The continuity of competence and aptitude is ensured through transmitting vital skills, industry insights, and experiential wisdom through mentoring relationships.

The corporate world is packed with obstacles, but with the help of a mentor, you can find your way through them. SheEOs play the role of mentors by providing advice, drawing on their own experiences, and offering ideas on overcoming challenges. Mentoring helps the next generation face professional obstacles head-on by teaching them to think strategically and resiliently.

Developing self-confidence and independence in young people is crucial for their advancement. Personalized guidance and constructive feedback provided by mentors can boost the self-assurance of upcoming leaders. SheEOs foster these skills in their mentees through mentoring programs, urging them to voice their opinions, take risks, and be bold in their professional pursuits.

Mentorship is a powerful tool for overcoming gender preconceptions and shattering glass ceilings. By actively mentoring others, SheEOs question long-held assumptions about what it means to be a leader and how women have historically been disadvantaged. By actively empowering individuals, we can create a more varied and inclusive professional environment.

Mentorship establishes a foundation for succession planning and guarantees that good leadership will continue sustainably. There will be a steady supply of competent leaders in the future because SheEOs are helping equip today's youth with the knowledge and experience to lead. This method ensures that organizations can continue to grow and thrive.

Mentorship promotes an attitude of continuous learning and adaptability. The role of sheets as role models encourages the next generation to be adaptable, creative, and open to new ideas as the corporate world changes. Organizations achieve long-term success when mentorship empowers their employees.

SheEOs greatly influence the creation of a mentorship culture within their workplaces. The organization's advocacy of mentorship programs teaches a culture of support and empowerment. This systemic assistance creates a more cheerful and nurturing atmosphere at work.

A mentorship relationship can be a gateway to new professional experiences and networking opportunities, broadening one's horizons. By serving as role models and mentors, SheEOs help the next generation gain exposure to essential people, industry events, and networks, giving them a leg up in their careers.

When led by SheEOs, mentorship encourages diversity and inclusiveness, creating a tapestry of perspectives. Mentorship fosters a diverse array of ideas and approaches by enabling individuals from different backgrounds and with varying points of view. A more innovative and adaptable workforce is a result of this variety.

Mentorship is a social responsibility that invests in the future. SheEOs' dedication advances the more significant social objective of producing competent, ethical leaders to empower the subsequent generation. Organizations are seen as change-makers when they commit to social responsibility.

A dedication to the long-term viability and advancement of the corporate world is at the heart of the connection between mentoring and empowering the next generation, mainly through the guidance of SheEOs. Emerging leaders can be empowered through mentorship in three ways: information transmission, leadership growth, and removing gender stereotypes. Recognizing their critical role, SheEOs work to leave a legacy of strong, successful women who will lead businesses into the future by being inclusive, innovative, and resilient.

12 STRATEGIES TO BUILDING AN INCLUSIVE SUCCESS ECOSYSTEM: SHEEOS MAKING IT POSSIBLE FOR WOMEN TO SUCCEED IN BUSINESS

In the mission to empower women and break down gender barriers, SheEOs are crucial in building a community that supports women in business. This is about more than just personal achievement; it's about creating a world where all women, regardless of background or expectations, can succeed, make a difference, and take the lead. This article delves into how SheEOs actively create and sustain a nurturing environment.

1. Promoting a Climate of Acceptance and Diversity:

Women in Executive Positions (SheEOs) actively promote diversity and inclusion within their organizations due to their leadership roles. This is more than lip service; it's a calculated effort to make women feel like they belong and are essential to the company's success.

2. Women-Specific Mentorship Programs:

Women in Executive Positions (SheEOs) know that mentoring can change lives, particularly when customized to help women overcome the obstacles they encounter in the corporate world. Mentorship programs are actively established and supported by them. These programs empower prospective women leaders with assistance, insights, and a network.

3. Promoting Chances for Networking:

For women to advance in their careers, networking is essential, and SheEOs use their connections to open doors for other women in business. These networking initiatives increase the visibility of women in business, promote collaboration, and break down isolation through industry events, seminars, or informal gatherings.

4. Gender-Inclusive Policy Implementation:

The execution of gender-inclusive policies by SheEOs is a beautiful example of equality in action. This encompasses anti-discrimination policies, parental leave policies, flexible work arrangements, and equal pay rules. Such regulations pave the way for women to achieve their career objectives without encountering obstacles.

5. Developing Talent:

SheEOs put money into initiatives that help women in their businesses become more skilled since they know this is essential to empowering women. Giving people the chance to attend seminars, classes, or other educational events that help them develop personally and professionally is one way to achieve this goal.

6. Establishing Secure Environments for Teamwork:

Fostering an atmosphere where women feel comfortable expressing themselves and sharing their thoughts, SheEOs promotes open dialogue. To achieve this goal, we must establish safe spaces where women can speak their minds and work together without fear of reprisal. Creating these secure areas promotes creativity and gives people a sense of agency as a group.

7. Confronting Implicit Prejudice:

By aggressively addressing unconscious biases inside their organizations, SheEOs strive to educate and sensitize their colleagues. A more equal workplace can be achieved by implementing educational initiatives, training sessions, and awareness programs that promote recognizing, understanding, and eliminating biases.

8. Working Together with Businesses Owned by Women:

Economic Empowerment: SheEOs understand the significance of bolstering the ecosystem by supporting women-run firms. They always look for new ways to collaborate, form collaborations, or buy from female-owned businesses. Beyond the scope of individual groups, this cooperative strategy helps women achieve economic independence.

9. Promoting Fair Representation:

The advocacy of SheEOs goes beyond their organizations to shape industry standards. They help bring about a more significant social change towards appreciating and acknowledging women's achievements in business by participating in forums, industry groups, and campaigns encouraging equal participation.

10. Facilitating Access to Assets:

The goal of SheEOs is to eliminate obstacles that women may have when trying to obtain resources crucial to their business ventures. Funding, mentorship, educational resources, and networks that women may have had a more challenging time navigating could be part of this solution.

11. Encouragement by Acknowledgment:

SheEOs zealously honor the accomplishments of women both inside their own companies and in the industry as a whole. They cultivate an environment that encourages others to strive for greater heights by highlighting the achievements of women and highlighting them as role models. This helps to establish a culture that values and celebrates the successes of women.

12. Dedication to Harmonizing Work and Personal Life:

Recognizing the significance of work-life integration, SheEOs pledge to provide a setting where women may successfully manage their personal and professional lives. This dedication helps with retention and adds to the happiness and contentment of women in the workplace.

As a company, SheEOs is dedicated to changing the story of success by building an environment where women may thrive. To create a corporate climate where women can flourish and become influential leaders and change agents, SheEOs promote diversity, offer mentorship, create networking opportunities, and tackle structural issues. To create a future free of the obstacles that have kept women from reaching their full potential and where an inclusive and supportive business ecosystem grows, this all-encompassing strategy for empowerment,

spearheaded by SheEOs, is crucial.

CHAPTER 7

Holistic Approach to Staying Well

A person's health and happiness might take a hit in the relentless pursuit of financial achievement. Recognizing the significance of overall performance, SheEOs actively pursue ways to stay healthy while juggling the challenges of the corporate world. By taking this tack, we can encourage resiliency on an individual level and pave the way for a more inclusive business environment for women.

Making Self-Care a Priority:

The tone is set by SheEOs who prioritize self-care and lead by example. This includes making time for activities that promote physical and mental health, such as exercising regularly, getting enough sleep, and practicing mindfulness as part of their daily routine. By demonstrating the importance of self-care, SheEOs promote a work environment where employees prioritize their health and happiness.

How to Set Appropriate Limits:

Establishing healthy boundaries is crucial for SheEOs to balance their personal and professional responsibilities. Avoiding burnout requires learning to delegate, having reasonable expectations, and knowing when to step back. In addition to encouraging a culture that respects work-life balance, setting limits helps people stay healthy in the long run.

Promoting Clear Communication:

Promoting a Positive Work Environment: SheEOs vigorously push for honest discussion around health and wellness in their companies. Employees can seek help without fear of stigma when they work in an environment that promotes open communication about mental health, stress, and other personal issues.

Offering Relief for Mental Health:

SheEOs put money into mental health support tools for their employees. Counseling services, Employee

Assistance Programs (EAPs), and stress management seminars fall under this category. Organizations prioritizing employee well-being show they care about their employee's mental health and overall wellness by offering accessible services.

Adaptable Work Schedules:

Women in Executive Positions (SheEOs) advocate for work-life integration by supporting flexible work arrangements that enable individuals to juggle their responsibilities. Workers report higher levels of job satisfaction and health when given more control over their work schedules, whether through reduced workweeks, more flexible hours, or the chance to work remotely.

Fostering a Holistic Company Culture:

SheEOs proactively support a positive company culture that prioritizes the happiness of its employees. A dedication to building a welcoming and inclusive workplace must harmonize with the organization's core principles for this to be achieved. Employees' happiness, engagement, and morale can only rise in an environment that values their health and wellness.

Funding Career Advancement:

Women in Executive Positions understand that ongoing education benefits one's career and personal health and happiness. One way to take care of one's health in all its aspects is to put money into professional development programs that teach people new things, make them more resilient, and provide them chances to grow as people.

Developing Mindfulness Routines:

SheEOs promote taking breaks and practicing mindfulness at work. Methods like meditation, deep breathing, and brief breaks to refuel workers might be part of the solution. You can reduce stress and improve your well-being by reflecting on these moments.

Recognizing Accomplishments:

Women in Executive Positions (SheEOs) take an active role in commemorating accomplishments and significant anniversaries within their companies. A pleasant and inspiring environment is enhanced by acknowledgment, which raises morale. An environment where people feel appreciated is conducive to general well-being, and SheEOs create that by recognizing and celebrating achievements.

Fostering a Balance Between Work and Personal Life:

Instead of advocating for rigid separation, SheEOs promote work-life harmony. To do this, one must acknowledge the inseparability of one's professional and personal lives and rally behind causes that aim to bring the two realms closer together. The end effect is a setting where people can thrive professionally without sacrificing health and happiness.

To create a supportive ecosystem for women in business, SheEOs prioritize strategies for sustaining well-being amidst work responsibilities. While building resilience, SheEOs prioritize self-care, set healthy boundaries, encourage open communication, and invest in tools that help mental and physical health. This not only helps their teams succeed holistically but also shapes the culture of their organizations. The strategy lays the groundwork for a corporate culture where women can flourish and lead with purpose and fulfillment by balancing professional obligations with personal well-being. This, in turn, adds to individual pleasure.

SUCCEEDING IN THE BUSINESS WORLD: SHEEOS NURTURING SUCCESS AND HAPPINESS

To thrive in the complex corporate environment, one must master the art and science of professional success and personal well-being. The function of SheEOs is vital in creating a peaceful environment for the firm and its employees, as they are the guardians of this corporate garden. Here, we take a look at how SheEOs promote a flourishing culture in the corporate garden, tying the success of the company to the happiness of its employees:

Encouraging a Culture Driven by Purpose:

Achieving success starts with having a well-defined goal to strive for. SheEOs foster a mission-driven culture by ensuring that the company's principles align with its more significant objective. Staff members report higher levels of job satisfaction and overall happiness when they can have a positive impact through their work.

Putting Money Into Staff Training:

To foster growth, SheEOs know that an organization's success depends on the individual's personal and professional development. They put money into programs that help employees grow professionally by giving them access to mentors and other resources for ongoing education and skill development. This dedication nurtures a mutually beneficial relationship between the company and its employees.

Advancing Diversity and Inclusion:

The corporate garden thrives on diversity, which creates a tapestry of perspectives. SheEOs advocate for diversity and inclusion because they know that different viewpoints strengthen innovation and resilience. The SheEOs plant a garden that rejoices in diversity by creating an environment where everyone feels welcome and appreciated.

Building an Ecosystem That Can Support It:

SheEOs know that a nurturing environment is crucial for the success of both individuals and organizations. Fostering a culture where employees feel supported in their quest for well-being, providing resources for mental health assistance, and advocating for work-life integration are all part of this.

Building Collaboration:

Achieving success is not something you do alone; it's a path you take with others. Within their organizations, SheEOs vigorously promote cooperation and collaboration. By fostering an environment where people play to one another's strengths and collaborate on projects, SheEOs can grow a corporate garden where everyone can thrive.

Clearly Outlining Objectives and Expectations:

By outlining clear objectives and goals, SheEOs guide growth and ensure everyone develops. Having clear and consistent conversations around corporate goals, individual responsibilities, and expectations is essential.

With everyone's expectations in front of them, employees can confidently navigate their growth in a controlled setting.

Recognizing and Honoring Significant Occasions:

In the corporate garden, SheEOs joyfully commemorate accomplishments and landmarks, creating a blossoming of recognition. A pleasant and inspiring environment is enhanced by acknowledgment, which raises morale. A culture where employees feel their efforts are valued is fostered by SheEOs through the recognition and celebration of triumphs, promoting an environment of continual growth.

Inspiring a State of Adaptability and Flexibility:

Amidst the ever-changing corporate landscape, SheEOs are cognizant that blossoming is possible. They believe that pivoting and embracing change is essential for human and organizational flourishing, so they foster adaptability and flexibility. The garden's ability to adapt guarantees its continued success, regardless of changes in the business scene.

Motivating People to Think Long-Term:

A mindset focused on growth is necessary for flourishing. SheEOs work tirelessly to provide an environment that rewards resiliency and lifelong education. Inspiring a growth mentality that sees obstacles as chances to learn and improve, SheEOs plant the seed that will eventually become even more remarkable achievements.

Impact Seeds:

To promote blossoming, SheEOs plant the seeds of Corporate Social Responsibility. Companies coached by SheEOs become more than just a success story; they help make the world better by funding projects that benefit locals and the environment.

Serving as a Guide and Mentor:

Developing future leaders is a part of nurturing seedlings and ensuring their success. Women in executive positions often serve as role models and advisors to others in their companies. A solid corporate garden, thriving with fresh leaders, may be nurtured by SheEOs through delivering ideas, sharing experiences, and fostering talent.

A Fertile Ground for Development:

SheEOs protect the culture of the organization. They foster an atmosphere of mutual regard, cooperation, and trust. The foundation upon which an organization and its members can build strong and prosperous futures is its culture.

SUSTAINABLE LONG-TERM SUCCESS: HOW TO GROW YOUR COMPANY'S GARDEN WITH THE HELP OF SHEEOS

A strategic and futuristic mindset is necessary for long-term business success. A SheEO's role as a visionary leader is to chart a course for the organization's future growth and prosperity. To ensure long-term success in the business garden, SheEOs use the following ten all-encompassing strategies:

1. Planting the Seeds of Vision:

By expressing an inspiring and distinct vision for the company, SheEOs set the stage for long-term success. In keeping with the principles and objectives of the organization, this vision acts as a compass. By establishing a solid foundation for all endeavors, SheEOs foster an environment conducive to deliberate and long-term expansion.

2. Developing the Organization's Talent Pool:

SheEOs understand that the organization's success is closely related to nurturing its talent pool. They put money into extensive programs to train employees' talents, encouraging a mindset of lifelong learning and the development of strong leaders. Success, in the long run, is guaranteed by SheEOs because they tend to a garden of competent and self-reliant persons.

3. Promoting Creativity:

SheEOs encourage creativity, which is essential for long-term success. They establish an environment that fosters innovation, experimentation, and taking chances. When she plants the seeds of innovation, they tend to a garden where the company can grow and change to meet the challenges of a dynamic marketplace.

4. Developing Strong Relationships with Stakeholders:

Sustainable success cannot be attained in a vacuum; it must attend to interrelated roots. Relationship building and stakeholder involvement are SheEOs' top priorities. Building solid relationships with clients, workers, financiers, and neighbors is essential. The resilience and health of the corporate garden are guaranteed by the SheEOs' diligent attention to these interdependent roots.

5. Promoting Growth through Diversity and Inclusion:

Successful Women in Executive Positions (SheEOs)
Know That Diversity Is Crucial To Long-Term Success.
Recognizing that a diverse garden is better able to

withstand pressure and change, they work hard to foster an inclusive and diverse work environment for all employees. A dedication to diversity can be a boon to development and prosperity in the long run.

6. Responsibilities to Society and the Environment:

Integrating environmental and social responsibility into the very essence of the organization, SheEOs foster ethical practices. A corporate garden that flourishes inside and leaves a positive and lasting impact on the world can be enabled by SheEOs through adopting sustainable business practices, reducing environmental impact, and positive societal contributions.

7. Being able to adjust and persevere when faced with change:

Staying Strong in Challenging Times: One must adapt to new circumstances to achieve long-term success. To help their businesses weather storms, overcome obstacles, and grab chances, SheEOs foster a culture of resilience and adaptation. Because of its adaptability, the corporate garden may thrive despite environmental changes.

8. The Role of Technology in the Digital Era:

Adopting New Technologies: Women in Executive Positions spearhead their companies' adoption of new technologies and digital transformation. They grow a garden that is efficient and ready to thrive in the ever-changing digital world by combining state-of-the-art technology with automation and data-driven insights.

9. Managing Risk at a Strategic Level:

SheEOs safeguard the organization's well-being and durability using strategic risk management methods. This requires foreseeing possible dangers, planning ways to lessen their impact, and training one's mind to see dangers not as threats but as possibilities for advancement. In the long term, SheEOs guarantee success by actively caring for the garden's health.

10. Gathering Knowledge from Past Experiences:

SheEOs foster a learning and adaptable company culture. To do this, one must draw insight from their good and bad experiences. To ensure long-term success in the dynamic business environment, SheEOs plant the seed of a growth mindset within their organizations and encourage constant learning and development.

:

Sustaining success in the corporate garden is ensured by the strategic foresight and leadership of SheEOs, who implement these long-term gardening tactics. A SheEO creates an atmosphere where the firm may succeed now and in the future by investing in people, encouraging innovation, building partnerships, and using responsible practices.

A LEGACY OF SUSTAINABLE SUCCESS: THE SHEEO'S MESSAGE OF ONGOING CONFIDENCE AND GROWTH

The thread of continuous confidence and growth in the fabric of SheEOs' sustainable success is a tribute to visionary leadership and a dedication to developing thriving corporate environments. Organizational guardians and SheEOs know that success isn't a destination but a process that calls for ever-evolving self-assurance and development. Here, we explore the core values that embody SheEO's commitment to fostering self-assurance and personal development for long-term success:

Promoting a Learning Environment:

The foundation of self-assurance and personal development is a mindset open to new information and ideas; sheets know this. Every difficulty is a chance to learn, adapt, and grow in an atmosphere that SheEOs create by fostering a hunger for knowledge and a commitment to continual improvement. This dedication to a learning culture supports maintaining a leadership position in the industry and being ready to handle the complexity of a dynamic business environment.

Guidance and Support for Personal Growth:

As they actively work to empower individuals through leadership and mentorship, mentoring becomes a foundational aspect of SheEOs' legacy. The next generation of leaders is licensed and given a road map to long-term success by SheEOs who share their stories, wisdom, and experiences. In this way, the mentoring legacy becomes a never-ending circle, with each generation carrying on the organization's guiding principles and lore.

Promoting Diversity and Inclusion:

Diversity and inclusion are the fertilizer that keeps self-assurance and progress growing in a successful garden. SheEOs know that various viewpoints foster new ideas and fresh approaches. The SheEOs plant the seeds for continued self-assurance and long-term success by cultivating an open space where all opinions are considered and respected. This diversity-rich corporate garden will eventually bear fruit.

Embracing Change and New Ideas:

Embracing adaptation and fostering innovation are essential components of continued success, and leading by example, they train themselves to view change as a springboard for improvement rather than a danger. Inspiring trust in the face of ambiguity, SheEOs keep their organizations adaptable, creative, and open to change by fostering an innovation culture.

Funding the Health and Happiness of Workers:

Caring for the people who work for you is essential to SheEOs' heritage. Providing extensive wellness programs is one way that SheEOs foster an atmosphere where workers feel appreciated, supported, and encouraged to develop personally and professionally. A well-cared-for personnel is an enduring asset that helps the corporate garden thrive.

Laying the Groundwork for the Future

Consistent self-assurance and expansion are inseparably bound up with the organization's global influence, and SheEOs get it. With this dedication, the organization may gain the trust of its stakeholders and provide its members with a sense of purpose, which will lead to long-term growth and a positive influence.

Marking Important Occasions and Accomplishments:

The SheEO is known for its tradition of commemorating achievements, whether great or small. SheEOs foster a culture of recognition by recognizing accomplishments; this increases morale, builds confidence, and inspires continued progress. The corporate garden fosters an encouraging environment where people always push themselves to improve by making success celebrations a regular part of the day.

The Importance of a Growth Mindset:

As a cornerstone of a history of continuous self-assurance and advancement, SheEOs promotes a growth mentality. The SheEOs foster an environment where failures are not seen as obstacles but as stepping stones to success by urging people to see them for what they are: chances to learn and grow. This mentality propels an organization's self-assurance and capacity to adapt and succeed.

As a legacy of SheEOs, we are committed to the corporate garden's long-term success and fostering a culture of continuous confidence and progress. To ensure that the organization's success isn't just a one-time occurrence but an ongoing path of growth and prosperity, SheEOs promotes a learning culture, empowers through mentoring, embraces diversity, and invests in well-being. This legacy serves as a compass, directing the organization through the ups and downs of the business world. It leaves a lasting impression on the corporate world, symbolizing unshakable progress, ongoing confidence, and a dedication to a legacy beyond generations.

CONCLUSION

Women are the authors of their own stories in the world of professional success. They write tales of overcoming challenges, balancing multiple responsibilities with grace, and passionately pursuing their dreams.

The business world is a canvas where women paint bold strokes of innovation, transforming the industry with visionary ideas. They are the architects of possibility, skillfully navigating the intricate threads of ambition to create new pathways for success. This passage celebrates the women who dare to dream, turn their passions into symphonies of triumph, and shatter ceilings, leaving behind an inspiring legacy that resonates throughout history. To all the women who are carving out a path of their own, know that your resilience, determination, and creativity inspire us all.

We celebrate the collective strength of women in business, honoring their resilience, innovation, and courage to lead where others have not dared to go. Each chapter is a testament to the unexplored territories conquered, the shattered glass ceilings and the positive impact on communities through the compassionate leadership of women who understand that true success is not a solo mission.

We're inviting all the fantastic SheEOs to join us in spreading empowerment throughout the community.

Let's work together to create positive change and help each other succeed. By participating in inspiring initiatives, providing mentorship, and advocating for change, we can make a difference and inspire others to follow their dreams. So come on, let's be the catalysts for change and help nurture ambition in all those around us!"